The Garden

Christina Hearne

BookLeaf Publishing

India | USA | UK

Presentation by *BookLeaf Publishing*

Web: www.bookleafpub.com

E-mail: info@bookleafpub.com

ISBN : 9789357448673

First edition 2021

DEDICATION

I would like to dedicate this book to my family. Especially to my late grandparents who I know would be proud to hold this book in their hands.

ACKNOWLEDGEMENT

I want to thank Jason, my husband and friend, for encouraging me to write and for being a wonderful father to our two daughters, Arianna and Maraiya. Thank you to my family for enjoying the poems I often wrote in their birthday cards and especially for my Mom and sister who always said I could write a book someday. And thank you to my friends and family who proofread and allowed me to share my work with them.

PREFACE

Beep...Beep...Beep.

The heart monitor measuring my Grandfather's rhythm was slowly changing. He had just been taken off the intubation that had been keeping him alive for the past several days. Infection had begun to make itself known after what had already been a long and tiring fight. It was time to say goodbye.

Beep......Beep..........beep.

I didn't quite know what all the waves and dips meant but I saw that they were becoming more irregular and not nearly as strong. Looking around the room I saw so many loved ones. My Mom and Dad, sisters, aunts, uncles and more. So many had been in this room to show their love and support, it was impossible to remember them all. Old army buddies, friends both new and old, brothers, children and grandchildren. All had taken a turn to come to this room, to say hello and eventually, goodbye.

Yet there was a joyful sorrow in the midst of everything. Though we had lost one of our dearest friends, we had been introduced to many more. Stories upon stories began to unfurl. Of days when my grandfather caused mischief in his local community groups to heroic operations in his days as an Air Force Medic.

I began to realize in even deeper clarity, how beautifully life and death can be paired. How often grief and love come together. And just how strange it is that we can somehow call such a tragic pain, blessed.

I still miss my Grandpa Carrillo, but oh how I smile when I think of how safe I felt in his country home. In the mobile home he had worked so long and hard for. Looking up at the endless sky of stars and listening to the night come alive. Remembering the moths that danced around the old yellow porch light and the foxes that came out after sunset to look for scraps of the evening meal or pieces of the fresh deer caught out on his land. I learned to love the balance of life.

Day to night,
dark and light.
The fawn just born,
and warmth it mourns.
A seed planted in spring,

now a beautiful thing.
And a heart that'd seen war,
came to all things adore.

This book comes from that odd balance I have seen. Life is often brutal, cruel and unfair, but it can also be beautiful, breathtaking and mesmerizing. Each side has its turn and indeed it will turn. But the butterfly is worth waiting for, even if many caterpillars have died trying to get there. The flower that opens is worth planting, even if it will fade soon after blooming. Beauty and joy are always worth searching for, even as tragedy tries to convince us of its permanence.

I will not be the best writer that you've ever read but I hope that I can remind you to seek the light when you are in darkness, to feel some warmth when you've been cold for so long and to find love for something when you feel lost and alone. Be strong my friend, a turn is coming, just keep looking for it.

The Garden

I planted a garden in my heart
And watered it with my tears,
And filled it with the memories
Of many long-past years.

Walking in, there I see
A sign that beckons "Enter",
To come thou in and sit a while
And find the Garden's center.

For in it lies such precious things
And it's where this first begins,
With one small tree that now has grown,
Filled with friends and kin.

Look now at the front
Where first you see the brights,
The brilliant moments, the hopeful thoughts
Of pinks and reds and whites.

This path is easy and filled with stones
Carved from many who've passed this way
The cairns mark the best known moments
Here they come to collect a bouquet.

But look and now I see still more
Some trails that walk the earth,
Without a guide, without paved stones
Where there is loss and dearth.

But still I walk, though carefully tread,
Through the unmarked paths
For therein lie the most tender shoots
But they're firm and holding fast.

This Garden is a strange sort of place
Where tears come together with laughter,
Where the mulch may smell and the thorn pricks
first
But you see the roses after.

But do not fear, for it is truly sweet,
To know the Garden of our hearts,
To love it when strong and love it when weak,
Our own precious work of art

The Forget-Me-Not

Silent stones sit keeping vigil
Over old flowers and grassy sod,
With names deeply carved and tenderly traced
Of dates and prayers to God.

Walking here feels quite serene
A place of peace and quiet,
Of lives once lived and love well gived
And I can't help but revere the silent.

I brought fresh flowers and here I lay
Them down on polished graveside wood,
A forget-me-not for my past loves,
As if I ever could.

A Single Flower

This flower sits in pretty prose
With beauty wafting still and slow
Where it will plant I still know not
But how I'll watch it as it grows.

And now I place it in a pot
A foreign flower, a rainbow caught
And while I watch, it gently sleeps
Rests from the day so fiercely fought.

Oh dear flower, you I'll keep
For no other like you will I reap
Hush now baby, don't you weep
I will hold you as you sleep.
Hush now darling, hush and sleep.

Milkweed

Persistent and unyielding,
You come and go each year,
With winter fall then spring arise
With seeds the wind blew here.

Taking shallow root, you still grow tall
And I wonder how you stand,
When nothing but a tiny tug
Could tear you from this land.

But still you grow and still you fight
To touch the light of day
And by your very life provide,
A place for some to stay.

The unyielding worm eats at your growth
And bear it still you do,
And grow in even greater ways
Before the season's through,

Oh how I hope to be like you
And come back from what tears,
To prove that pushing toward the light
Will overcome despairs.

Orange Blossoms

The chill of December breaks its hold
With the precious scent of fruit,
Reminding me of that yearly moment
Collecting nature's loot.

Pulled from the tree and twisted free
Its heft weighs with Eden's taste,
I've collected a hundred, no two hundred more,
So as not to leave a waste.

The cold of winter stays at bay
Under my long clothes cover,
And my Mom and Dad are here with me,
Bringing one bag after another.

We bless our neighbors and make some juice
With all our fragrant bounty,
We have the best tree on our street
Or maybe in the county.

But I've moved away and instead I wait
At the lonely market stand,
Smelling the fruit I once picked myself
With loving family hands.

Two dollars now, for just one pound
I sigh and return it to the stack,
Wishing here, now yet again,
I had those old days back.

For money won't make memory
And the house has long been sold,
And the welcome chill of after fall,
Now just seems long and cold.

One more glance at the vendor's booth,
To close my eyes and sustain,
because the scent of an orange blossom,
has brought me home again.

The Hummingbird

Busy, busy, busy
You never see your shine,
Busy, busy, busy
O small creature divine.

On wings of wind and tiny toes,
With glossy wings and nectar nose,

You flit and flutter to and fro,
Thinking of where you next will go.

You feed your young and migrate south
Always zooming all about,

As if each moment was yours to bear
And waste it not or else despair.

If you looked out, perhaps you'd see.
The smile your very presence frees,

Be still small bird, tomorrow will come
Whether or not you still do hum,

Busy, busy, busy
Come and see your shine,

Busy, busy, busy,
O small creature divine.

Moon Garden

Night has fallen
The sun has left,
Two worlds divided
By twilight cleft.

Here in the dark
Now something stirs,
Is it bright eyes lurking
With predatory purrs?

Or perhaps a shade
Of old memory,
Making me fearful
Of what I don't see.

I draw into myself
And close tight my eyes,
Not wanting to see
What brings my demise.

Yet hearing nothing
I open them slow,
And before me there,
An unusual glow.

It floats on the air
Tiny and light,
So I reach out my hand
In the dark of the night.

It lands and tickles,
Finally I see,
A small firefly
Here just for me.

I stare in wonder
And off it flies,
Now I see more
As I bid it good-bye.

Only in the night
can I now see,
The light of the stars,
Shimmering on the trees.

The primrose has opened,
A flower I thought still,
And where bees once drank,
Come moths for their fill.

This land is alive,
At a time I thought dead,
It has become my Moon Garden
Quite sacred instead.

Sitting by Reflective Waters

When the water is stirred or a stone thrown in,
I see the distortion
not without, but within.

So I then think myself the one that is curved,
And knowing that image,
Leaves me unnerved.

Convinced I am broken,
Though truly I'm not.
Convinced I'm outcast,
Though I know I am sought.

I look up and see perfect faces and forms,
But look down and see
A reflection forlorn.

Who is this stranger staring at me?
Am I really the rippled face
I think I may be?

But look, it calms
And for a moment I see,
That now I'm something
I used to dream I would be.

My fine lines are stories,
My shade a people,
My smile a joy,
My necklace a steeple.

Another stone's thrown in
But now I know,
That without the roiling,
The truth would show.

So whether under falls
Or besides waters still,
I'm still loved and worthwhile,
And have a role to fill.

Watching clouds

O where do you go in silent flight?
Down to the valleys and up on the heights?
Sailing through skies in greys and whites,
Reflecting the colors of changing light.

Your evening hues are like the bay,
That dance with warmth at the end of the day,
Within you my mind is free as fay,
A place to dream and think and play.

You roil with rain and dance with thunder
Lighting the skies and tearing asunder,
Bringing to Earth awe and wonder,
Flawless art, without any blunder.

You shade my garden and give it life
To save it from the scorching knife,
To save it from the heat and strife,
And give it strength like drum and fife.

Watching clouds, I see them go,
In shifting shapes both high and low.
O when will I dance in that meadow,
Free to fly and free to glow?

O where do you go in silent flight?
Down to the valley and up on the heights?
For now I'll wait with earthen scars,
Riding planes and wishing on stars.

Storm of Wonder

My feet are grounded here in this place
A place I know, a field I can trace
I know every pebble, I see each crack
I know every flower, reds, blues and black.

But in my eyes are blue rings of wonder
Looking up at the sky and the distant thunder.
The roiling storms, the wonderful wind
And I wait eagerly for the show to begin.

It captures my mind, this force of the sky
It fills my Garden and opens my eyes.
Sailing with lightning and riding with hail,
My heart of fantasy, it does avail.

I breathe in the smell of coming rain,
And marvel at the tempest once again,
Powerful and unyielding, I can't control
Whether it brings life or destruction as the
thunder rolls.

But trust I have, for faith has been true,
And storms that come, all bring something new.
So I'm awed by the clouds of gathering dark

For their strength is drawn from the highest
Monarch.

And He is still good, though trees may fall
Not that the crushing is good at all.
But within each storm I've seen something new
For trust I have in words that are true.

So come ye tempest, bring now the rain,
My foundation is strong, my roots are ingrained.

Barren Earth

Field of barren earth,
like a living canvas of
Endless potential

A World of Trees

A world full of trees,
and within every leaf
A thousand stories

The Broken Seed

I found a broken acorn,
And picked it from the mess,
That lay in piles all around,
Where others came to rest.

The shell is scratched and broken,
From where it chose to dwell,
Or perhaps made in the moment,
When from the tree it fell.

I held it tight and saw myself,
Within its fractured heart,
And went to hide it by a lake
Where it might risk to start.

Perhaps I'll return and find my seed,
Tall and green with life,
Thankful for the hurt it took,
Which opened it through strife.

The broken seed may seldom thrive,
But without the break it stays,
Only but a tiny seed
With restless, lonely days.

So grow my seed, grow strong and show
The tree you will become,
And I may see and so believe,
I too can overcome.

Grave In My Heart

The storm shook my house
It made me quake,
My own heart quivered
And tears made a lake.

It nearly drowned me
When I saw what I lost,
A price too high,
Beyond reasonable cost.

This child of mine
Taken too soon,
The hopes I had,
Now an empty room.

Yet love is strong
And love I hold,
For the precious child,
Never old.

So I'll plant a flower, carved on stone
And love you till it fades,
And find you always in my heart,
Come sun or somber shade.

Growing Pains

I am happy here
In this pot of mine,
A place I know
with walls so fine.

This place is sturdy,
It protects me from others,
I need no one here,
Not friends or brothers.

But wait! Why this pulling?
Something's amiss,
If I had wished for anything
It certainly wasn't this.

"Ow!" Says I.
"Stop this at once!
Are you truly a wiseman
Or simply a dunce?

It hurts, what you're doing,
Can't you please see,
That taking me from my pot,
Is a great pain to me."

Now what is this?
A hole in the ground?
But what of my safety,
Where I was rootbound?

There's much that can touch me,
There's much that can harm,
Well…I suppose the ground here
Has its own charm.

I thought it was scary
To be alone and free,
But my new soil taught me,
I was actually a tree.

I never would have grown
Beyond my small pot,
And those who remained
Are a pitiable lot.

In the new soil I've found,
That my roots can grow deep.
And now i have others
Who make me complete.

Visitors

A Garden is seldom made
From a single pair of hands,
It's given life through good advice,
That fertilize the lands.

And thereafter a haven
I think that it should be,
A place where many come to sit
And ponder what they see.

For what good is a Garden
If it remains hidden away,
Its flowers never knowing
New smiles everyday?

So come and walk the fields,
I'll learn how to be brave,
And let your eyes of wonder
Pick over what I've saved.

Things that I have suffered,
Things that I have earned,
Are all indeed quite useless,
If they're not also learned,

By the many people
Who have a place to build,
Whose Garden is just starting,
Whose soil is being tilled.

How do you grow a flower
In a place of pain?
How do you plant something
In a patch of heavy rain?

How does this thrive
When it's been eaten twice?
What good are these moments
If not for sound advice.

So come and visit,
Come and stay,
Ask about the Garden
And together, we'll pray.

What is a Gardener?

Think with me. What is a gardener?
A man of flesh and bone?
Who spends his extra time and days
In the dirt that makes him groan?

Or a dreamer yet who sees the world
As it may dare to be,
With colors of brilliant rainbow light,
Filled with life and glee?

If this is true it must be known
That not all gardeners make,
An earthen field with flora grown,
With toil and seeds and rake.

No indeed, can't you see,
There's so much more we do?
We teach a child, we raise a house,
We grow a business too.

We can paint a page of color,
That no one's seen before,
Or put some words together,
To touch a broken core.

We harbor a hope to see things grow
In whatever way they'll shine,
Taking seeds of what may be
And raising them so fine.

Not everyone will be in first
Nor every fruit so sweet,
But in the toil, the work and time
We find our living beat.

So we'll learn and grow day by day,
And never know it all,
But this world is even better still
For each kindness, great and small.

I Never Knew

I never knew the mountains
Could be so far and vast,
The valleys o so very deep
With rivers rushing past.

I never knew my parents
Could come to be my friends,
And grant me wisdom many times
From their own unique lens.

I never knew that travel
Would open up my eyes,
And each distinctive people group
Would make me realize,

That flowers bloom in many ways
In rain, or snow or shine,
Some looking different on the way
Yet equally divine.

I hope I leave a garden
That others come see,
And ponder life's most precious gifts
Under the family tree.

I never knew this life so grand,
could be so very wide,
And when I close my eyes at last
I'll whisper "What a ride!"

Sleeping Life

Little life, so fast asleep,
'Neath winter's blanket, dark and deep.
Silently dreaming, nary a peep,
Growing roots, like small white sheep.

Twilight sky begins to glow
And slowly grasses start to grow,
They call you from your sleep below,
Calling you to come and know.

"Wake" they say, "And taste the light,
See birds return from autumn's flight".
"Rise" They cry to the little sprite.
"Rise into the melting white."

It strived against the callous weed,
Until at last, its head was freed.
To bloom with joy from winter's need
And herald others to succeed.

Who's In The Garden?

Who lives in the garden?
Come take a look.
Perhaps an orb spider,
In a cozy nook.

Or maybe a moth
Out looking for food,
Enjoying grass music
When buzzing's subdued.

Or perhaps a shiny trail
Leading to a slug,
Passing mulch and fallen leaves
That cover doodlebugs.

And in the day, the tallest flowers
On which the hummers rest,
Share sweetness with the butterflies
And other tiny pests.

Come to feast now are the scales
That flash in brown and green,

Followed by the little birds
That come to stop and preen.

Sometimes a special guest comes in
A child so still and calm,
Looking out with wondrous eyes,
Shouting, "It's a jungle Mom!"

Left Shoe

A pesky rat did make a theft,
From my garden it did heft,
My left foot shoe
But I'm not askew,
Because at least my right is left.